IN THE SCHOOL OF
THE HOLY SPIRIT

IN THE SCHOOL
OF THE
HOLY SPIRIT •• Jacques Philippe

Translated by Helena Scott

 Scepter

CONTENTS

III .. How Can We Know That an Inspiration Comes from God? / 44

APPENDICES

I

II

III

IV

INTRODUCTION

My Jesus, it is truly easy to become holy; it just takes a little good will! And if He finds this minimum of good will in a soul, He quickly gives Himself to her. And nothing can stop Him, neither our faults nor our falls, absolutely nothing. Jesus hurries to help that soul; and if the soul is faithful to this grace from God, she can in a short time reach the highest level of holiness that a created being can attain here below. God is very generous and does not refuse His grace to anyone. He gives even more than we ask for. The shortest road is faithfulness to the inspirations of the Holy Spirit.

This beautiful text is taken from the diary of St. Faustina.[1] Even though it is simple and concise, it delivers an extremely important message for people who aspire to holiness—to people who want to respond as far as possible to God's love.

[1] *Petit journal de Soeur Faustine* (Marquain, Belgium: Jules Hovine), p. 142; English ed.: St. Faustina Kowalska, *Diary: Divine Mercy in my Soul* (Stockbridge, Mass.: Marians of the Immaculate Conception: 1999). Sister Faustina, who was born in 1905 and died on October 5, 1938, was beatified by Pope John Paul II on the Sunday after Easter 1993. She was canonized on Divine Mercy Sunday, April 30, 2000. This Polish religious received from Jesus the mission of making Divine Mercy better known in the world, especially by means of an icon of Christ's Mercy that she asked a painter to produce.

The major question for such souls, a question that sometimes causes them pain, is to know what to do about this message.

Maybe you never have been particularly concerned about this question. Maybe you never have aspired to love God as much as he possibly can be loved. If not, I ask that you now beg the Holy Spirit to put that desire in you, and even that you beg him to leave you restless until you have that aspiration. Then you will be really happy; for as our Lord said: "Blessed are those who hunger and thirst for righteousness, for they shall be satisfied!" [2]

For those who aspire to the fullness of love, every suggestion that shows them a clearer or quicker way to that goal is extremely valuable. Almost nobody realizes it, but in my opinion it is just as important to help devout people become even holier—and faster—as it is to help sinners be converted. It benefits the Church just as much. The world will be saved by the prayers of the saints.

This is why it is very important, even if not everyone understands, to pass on the best parts of the saints' messages to today's Christians in order to help them progress faster toward the perfection of love.

The key question in this process may be our not knowing where to focus our efforts. The answer isn't always apparent, nor is it what we might suppose at the outset.

[2] Matthew 5:6. In Scripture, righteousness or justice means, rather than the meaning it is commonly given, the attitude of people whose will is fully "adapted" to God's will, loving him and loving their neighbor. In other words, the scriptural term "righteousness" is what we understand as holiness.

St. Faustina, in the passage quoted above and also in some of the other reflections in her *Diary*, gives us an indication from her own experience that is worth paying attention to: the shortest way to holiness is *faithfulness to the inspirations of the Holy Spirit.* So, rather than scattering our efforts in areas of our lives where they might turn out to be sterile or unproductive, Sister Faustina proposes that we center them on this point: be alert to recognize, welcome, and put into practice the inspirations of the Holy Spirit. Faithfulness to such inspiration is by far the most "profitable" course.

Let's first consider why this is, and then try to see exactly what is involved.

I

HOLINESS IS THE WORK OF
THE HOLY SPIRIT

There is a widespread but mistaken idea that holiness is the work of human beings: that what we need is to have a clear program of perfection, set to work with courage and patience, and achieve it little by little. And that's all there is to it.

Unfortunately (or fortunately!) there is much more to it than that. It does take courage and patience, undoubtedly. But it is certainly not true that holiness is the result of a program of life we set ourselves. There are several reasons why holiness is not the work of human beings; here are two main ones.

I. THE TASK IS BEYOND OUR POWER

It is impossible to attain holiness by our own power. The whole of Scripture teaches us that it can only be the fruit of God's grace. Jesus tells us: "Apart from me, you can do nothing." [1] And St. Paul says: "I can will what is right, but

[1] John 15: 5.

I cannot do it."[2] The saints themselves witness to this. This is what St. Louis Grignon de Montfort says, speaking of this sanctification that is God's plan for us:

> What an admirable work: dust changed into light, filth into purity, sin into holiness, the creature into the Creator, and man into God! Admirable work, I repeat, but a work that is difficult in itself, and impossible for unaided nature! Only God, by his grace—abundant, extraordinary grace—can accomplish it; and the creation of the whole universe is not such a surpassing masterpiece as this.[3]

However great our efforts, we cannot change ourselves. Only God can get to the bottom of our defects, and our limitations in the field of love; only he has sufficient mastery over our hearts for that. If we realize that we will save ourselves a great deal of discouragement and fruitless struggle. We do not have to become saints by our own power; we have to learn how to let God make us into saints.

That does not mean, of course, that we don't have to make any effort; but if our efforts are not to remain fruitless, they must be directed to the right end. We should fight, not to attain holiness as a result of our own efforts, but to let God act in us without our putting up any

[2] Romans 7: 18.
[3] St. Louis Marie Grignon de Montfort, *The Secret of Mary*, beginning of the first part.

resistance against him; we should fight to open ourselves as fully as possible to his grace, which sanctifies us.

This opening of ourselves demands a great deal of humility because it means renouncing our tendency, born of pride, to want to manage by ourselves; it means accepting our own poverty and so on. But at the same time it is very encouraging.

The reason it is encouraging is that our own powers are limited, but God's power and love are not. And we unfailingly can obtain the help of that power and love for our weakness. All we have to do is peacefully recognize and admit the fact of our weakness, and place all our trust and hope in God alone. Basically, it's very simple; but like all simple things it takes years for us to understand and, above all, to practice.

The secret of holiness could be described as discovering that we can obtain everything from God, on condition that we know "how to get hold of him." That is the secret of St. Thérèse of Lisieux's little way: God has a father's heart, and we can unfailingly obtain what we need from him, if we know how to take him by the heart. Here is a passage from a letter by St. Thérèse of Lisieux that can help us to understand what this means:

> I want to try to make you understand, by a very simple comparison, how much Jesus loves those souls, even imperfect ones, who entrust themselves to Him. Imagine that a father has two

children who have been naughty and disobedient; and that when he comes to punish them, he sees one who trembles and runs away from him in terror, knowing in his heart that he deserves to be punished; and that his brother, instead, throws himself into his father's arms, telling him that he's sorry he has displeased him, he loves him, and to prove it he will be good from now on. Now if that child asks his father to punish him with a kiss, I believe that the happy father's heart will not be able to resist his son's filial trust, since he knows his sincerity and love. Yet he also knows that his son will fall into the same faults again, but he is always ready to forgive him if his son always appeals to his heart.[4]

I think St. Thérèse found this idea that we can obtain everything from God in the works of St. John of the Cross, who was virtually the only teacher she had. This is what he says in the *Spiritual Canticle*:

Great is the power and persistence of love, since it overcomes and binds God himself. Happy is the soul who loves, because that soul holds God captive, and obtains from him all that he or she desires. For God's nature is such that, if we take him

---

[4] St. Thérèse of Lisieux, Letter 258.

by love, in the right way, we will make him do what we want.[5]

This daring expression about the power that our love and trust can exercise over God's heart contains a beautiful and very deep truth. St. John of the Cross expresses it elsewhere in other terms: "What touches God's heart, and triumphs over it, is firm hope."[6] And, again:

God has such high esteem for the hope possessed by souls that are ceaselessly turned toward him and rely on him alone, that one can truly say that they obtain all that they hope for.[7]

Holiness is not a program for life, but something obtained from God. There are even infallible means for obtaining it, and the important thing is to know what they are. We all have the power to become holy, simply because God lets himself be won over by the trust we put in him. The aim of the following sections is to put us on the right track.

2. ONLY GOD KNOWS EACH PERSON'S ROAD

A second reason why we don't become holy simply by drawing up a plan for ourselves is that there are as many

[5] St. John of the Cross, *Spiritual Canticle B*, strophe 32, 1.

[6] St. John of the Cross, Maxim 112.

[7] St. John of the Cross, Maxim 119.

forms of holiness, and hence also ways to holiness, as there are people. For God, each person is absolutely unique. Holiness is not the realization of a given model of perfection that is identical for everyone. It is the emergence of an absolutely unique reality that God alone knows, and that he alone brings to fruition. No individual knows what his own holiness consists of. Holiness is only revealed to us by degrees, as we journey on, and it is often something very different from what we imagine, so much so that the greatest obstacle on the path to holiness may be to cling too closely to the image we have of our own perfection.

What God wants is always different, always disconcerting; but ultimately it is infinitely more beautiful, because only God is capable of creating totally unique masterpieces, while we humans can only imitate.

This uniqueness has an important consequence. To reach holiness, we cannot be content merely to follow the general principles that apply to everyone. We also need to understand what God is asking of us in particular, which he may not be asking of anyone else. How can we discover what it is? In different ways, naturally: through the happenings of our lives, in the advice of a spiritual director, and in many other ways as well.

Among these ways, there is one that is so fundamental and important that it merits an explanation: the inspirations of divine grace. In other words, the inner promptings, the movements of the Holy Spirit in the depths of our hearts by which God makes known to us what he is asking of us, and at the same time gives us the strength we need to accomplish it, at least if we consent. How we should discern and receive these inspirations will be discussed later.

To become holy, to become saints, we must of course try as hard as we can to do God's will as it comes to us in a general way that is valid for everyone: through Scripture, the Commandments, and so on. It is also indispensable, as has just been said, to go further: to aspire to know not only what God demands of everyone in general, but also what he wants more specifically of us individually. That is where the inspirations referred to above come in. These inspirations are necessary even to know God's general will for us.

The first reason for this is that if we aspire to perfection, we have so many things to tackle, so many commandments and virtues to practice, that it is impossible for us to fight on all fronts. And so it is important to know at any given moment which virtue we should give priority to, not according to our own ideas, but according to what God actually wants of us, because that is what will be infinitely more effective. And it isn't always what we may think. It can happen that we make superhuman efforts to improve on one point, while God is asking us for something else. For example, we may be making a supreme effort to correct a character defect, while what God is asking us to do is accept it with humility and gentleness toward ourselves! The inspirations of grace are invaluable in enabling us to direct our efforts correctly, among the many battles we have to wage. Without those inspirations, there is a serious danger that we may either let ourselves off too easily on certain points, or demand of ourselves more than God is demanding of us, which is just as bad, and more common than we might think. God calls us to perfection, but he is not a perfectionist. And perfection is reached not so much by external conformity to an ideal as by inner faithfulness to God's inspirations.

There is a second reason, shown by experience. Even though we know that God's will and commandments apply to everyone, we do not always have the strength to fulfill them. Now, every time we respond faithfully to a motion of the Spirit, out of a desire to be docile to what God expects of us, even if it's something almost insignificant in itself, that faithfulness draws grace and strength down on us. That strength can then be applied to other areas and may make us capable of one day practicing the commandments that up until then we had not been capable of fulfilling entirely. This could be seen as one application of the promise made by Jesus in the Gospel: "Well done, good and faithful servant; you have been faithful over a little, I will set you over much." [8] One can deduce a fundamental "spiritual law" from it: *We will obtain the grace to be faithful in the important things that at present*

[8] Matthew 25: 21.

20

we find impossible, by dint of being faithful in the little things within our grasp, especially when those little things are the ones that the Holy Spirit asks of us by calling to our hearts with his inspirations.

Finally, there is a consideration of capital importance that can motivate us to want to be faithful to these inspirations. If we decide to make an effort to achieve some spiritual progress according to our ideas and our own criteria, we are by no means sure to succeed. As we have seen, there is sometimes a big difference between what God is actually asking of us, and what we imagine he is asking. We won't have the grace to do what God is not asking of us. But for what he *is* asking, he has promised us his grace: God grants what he commands. When God inspires us to do something (if it really is God who is the source of that inspiration), at the same time he supplies the ability to do it, even if it is beyond our capacity or scares us at the start. Every motion that comes from God brings both the light to understand what God intends, and the strength to accomplish it: light that illuminates the mind, and strength that gives power to the will.

3. FAITHFULNESS TO GRACE DRAWS DOWN FURTHER GRACES

Here is a little story from Sister Faustina, again taken from her *Diary*.

> This evening I tried to do all my exercises before Benediction, because I felt sicker than usual. Right

after Benediction I was going to bed. But as I went into my cell, suddenly I felt inwardly that I had to go to Sister N.'s cell because she needed help. I went straight to her cell, and Sister N. said: "Oh, how good it is, Sister, that God sent you!" And she spoke in such a low voice that I could hardly hear her. She said: "Sister, please bring me a little tea with lemon, because I'm so thirsty and I can't move. I'm suffering so much." And she really was suffering a lot, and she had a high fever. I settled her more comfortably and quenched her thirst with a little tea. When I went back into my cell, my soul was penetrated with a great love for God and I understood that we should pay great attention to inner inspirations and follow them faithfully. And faithfulness to one grace attracts others.[9]

This text illustrates some of the things we have just looked at. It underlines a central point: each act of fidelity to an inspiration is rewarded by more abundant graces, especially by more frequent and stronger inspirations. The soul is drawn steadily on to greater faithfulness to God, a clearer perception of his will, and greater ease in accomplishing it. St. Francis de Sales says, likewise:

When we profit from an inspiration that our Lord sends, he then sends another, and thus our Lord

[9] St. Faustina, *Petit journal*, p. 282.

continues his graces as long as we continue to profit from them.[10]

And that is the fundamental dynamism that can lead us little by little to holiness, our faithfulness to grace drawing down other graces.[11] St. Thérèse of Lisieux also witnesses to this "dynamism of faithfulness" that makes accomplishing God's will progressively easier:

> The practice of virtue became sweet and natural to me; to begin with, my struggle often showed in my face, but little by little this disappeared and renunciation became easy to me even at the first moment. Jesus said this: "To everyone who has will more be given, and he will have abundance." For one grace that I received faithfully, he granted me a host of other. . . ."[12]

It should be added that this process is accompanied by the grace of joy: even though obeying the Holy Spirit is often hard for us at the start, because it conflicts with our fears, our attachments, and so forth, that obedience is always, in the end, a source of joy and happiness. It is accompanied by an outpouring of grace that enlarges

---

[10] Letter 2074 in the Annecy edition. Father Ravier, introducing the essential points of the spirituality of St. Francis de Sales, says: "Inspirations are one of the means the Holy Spirit uses to guide each person at every moment. The ability to discern and follow them is one of the most important points of the devout life": Francis de Sales, *Lettres d'amitié spirituelle* (Bruges: Desclée de Brouwer), p. 818.

[11] This does not mean that all is lost if at any time we are unfaithful to them. This point will be discussed further on.

[12] St. Thérèse of Lisieux, *Autobiography*, Manuscript A, folio 48.

our hearts and makes our souls feel free and happy to travel along the Lord's paths: "I will run in the way of thy commandments, when thou enlargest my understanding"! [13] God rewards us as generously as only he can. He treats us as only God can. Another spiritual law, which is worth taking note of and that is confirmed by experience, is this: this path of docility to the motions of the Holy Spirit may be very demanding, because "the Spirit breathes where he will," [14] but it is a path of freedom and happiness. We may journey without constraint, our hearts not confined but expanded. This enlarging of the heart is a clear sign of the presence of the Spirit.

The Holy Spirit is rightly called the Consoler. When the touches of the Spirit, enlightening us and impelling us to act, are well received, they pour into our hearts not just light and strength but solace and peace, that often fills us with consolation. This happens even when their object is something unimportant; because these touches proceed from the Holy Spirit they share in God's power to console and fulfill us.

Just a minute amount of the unction of the Holy Spirit can fill our hearts with more contentment than all the riches of the earth, because it shares in God's infinity. Richard of St. Victor says:

[13] Psalm 119[118]: 32.
[14] John 3: 8.

I boldly affirm that one single drop of these divine consolations can do what all the pleasures of the world cannot. The pleasures of this world cannot satisfy the heart; and one single drop of the inner sweetness that the Holy Spirit pours into the soul, delights it utterly and causes it a holy inebriation.

"Thou anointest my head with oil, my cup over-floweth," we read in Psalm 23[22]. And this unction of the Spirit is unfailingly spread in the souls of those who do the good that the Holy Spirit inspires in them. Here we find another great law of the spiritual life: what is really able to satisfy our hearts is not so much the gifts we receive as the good that God inspires and that we practice. There is more happiness in giving than in receiving.

We can see, then, how fruitful it is to welcome and follow the motions of the Spirit, to the point where we can say with Sister Faustina that this is the main means of our sanctification. Various questions arise from this. How can we recognize and distinguish these motions of the Spirit? Does everyone receive them? How often? How can we foster their presence in our spiritual life?

It is worth looking at the last of these questions first.

II

HOW CAN WE
FOSTER INSPIRATIONS?

God loves everyone with unique love; he wants to lead them all to perfection, but at the same time has very different paths for different people. This means that the frequency and the characteristics of the inspirations of grace will differ from one person to another. We cannot force the Spirit, and God is the master of his gifts.

That said, it cannot be doubted that God will grant each person at least the inspirations he needs for his own sanctification. This is what St. Francis de Sales says:

Those who keep their hearts open to holy inspirations are happy! For they will never lack those that they need in order to live in their state well and devoutly, and to exercise the duties of their profession in a holy way. For as God gives, by way of nature, to each animal the instincts that are required for its conservation and for the exercise of its natural properties, so too, if we do not resist

God's grace, he gives each of us the inspirations we
need in order to live, act, and maintain ourselves in
the spiritual life.[1]

It should also be added that these motions of the Spirit
(even though, unfortunately, they have little place in the
lives of many Christians) are not something exceptional in
themselves, but form part of the "normal functioning" of
the spiritual life.

St. Paul suggests this when he says: "All those who are
led by the Spirit of God are the sons of God,"[2] and also:
"If we live by the Spirit, let us also walk by the Spirit."[3]
We have all received adoption as children of God and the
grace of the Holy Spirit in Baptism. The normal fruit of
this Sacrament is the germinating in our lives of what
theology terms the "gifts of the Holy Spirit," whose aim is
to "prepare the soul to follow promptly the impulse of
divine inspiration."[4] St. Thomas also says: "The gifts of
the Holy Spirit render all the faculties of the soul capable
of submitting to the motions of God."[5]

Every Christian should desire and pray for these inspirations of grace. Of course, God grants them in greater or
lesser measure, and "From everyone to whom much is

---

[1] St. Francis de Sales, *Treatise on the Love of God*, book 8, chap. 11; trans. H. B.
Mackey (London: Burns Oates & Washbourne, 1884).

[2] Romans 8: 14.

[3] Galatians 5: 25.

[4] St. Thomas Aquinas, *Summa theologiae*, IaIIae, q. 68, a. 1.

[5] Ibid.

given, much will be required"; [6] and those to whom less is given will have less asked of them.

But it remains true that inspirations are not an optional extra in spiritual life, because they can be decisive for spiritual progress, and it is a matter of the greatest importance to welcome them into our lives.

What specifically will enable inspirations of grace to take place in us? What can we do so that God gives us the benefit of them as much as possible? There are a certain number of conditions that are conducive to their appearing in our souls.

I. PRACTICE PRAISE AND THANKSGIVING

What prevents us from receiving more abundant graces from God may be quite simply our not being sufficiently grateful and not thanking him for the graces he has already given us.

There is no doubt that if we thank God with all our heart for each grace received, especially for the inspirations, he will grant us more.

St. Thérèse of Lisieux said to her sister Céline:

What most draws down graces from our dear Lord is gratitude, for if we thank him for a gift, he is touched and hastens to give us ten more, and if we thank him again with the same sincerity, what an

[6] Luke 12: 48.

incalculable multiplication of graces! I have experienced this: try it and you will see. My gratitude for all that he gives me is boundless, and I prove this to him in a thousand ways.[7]

This should not be something calculated, but the result of realizing that ingratitude toward God imprisons us within ourselves and closes us to his grace. "Bless the Lord, O my soul, and forget not all his benefits!"[8] says the Psalm. Praise purifies the heart and prepares it marvelously to receive divine grace and the motions of the Holy Spirit.

2. DESIRE AND ASK FOR THEM

We must, of course, desire God's inspirations and ask for them frequently in prayer: "Ask, and it will be given you."[9] One of the petitions we make to God most often should be: "Inspire me in all my decisions, and never let me neglect any of your inspirations."

We should ask for them in all the circumstances of our lives. At more critical moments, when we are faced with important choices, or when we have the impression that our life with our Lord is limping a little and needs revivifying, it can be very good to go on retreat for a few days and pray more intensely for the light of the Holy Spirit.

---

[7] St. Thérèse of Lisieux, *Conseils et souvenirs*, collected by Sister Geneviève [her sister Céline] (Paris: Editions du Cerf, 1973).

[8] Psalm 103[102]: 2.

[9] Luke 11: 9.

It would be strange if God were then to refuse us his inspirations.

3. RESOLVE TO REFUSE GOD NOTHING

What matters even more than conscious, explicit prayer on this subject is that we should have a strong and constant *determination to obey God in everything*, big or little, without any exception. The more God sees this disposition of total docility in us, the more he will favor us with his inspirations.

This is not to say that in fact we must be able to obey God in absolutely everything: that is still something that is impossible for us to do because of our weakness. But we do have to be determined to do so, and do all in our power to ensure, particularly by prayer, that we keep strengthening our resolution not to neglect a single one of the wishes that God might express to us, no matter how small it is.

We should also be clear that this determination should not become a scruple that the devil could use to discourage us, a fear of "missing" God's will or not understanding it. In this area, as in everything, we should let ourselves be led by love and not by fear; and, as St. Francis de Sales used to say, we should "love obeying more than we fear disobeying." [10] We should strengthen ourselves continually in our resolution to be docile to God, mindful that the

---

[10] St. Francis de Sales, Letter to St. Jane Frances de Chantal.

devil never use our docility to get us upset or discouraged over our inevitable failures.

4. PRACTICE FILIAL AND TRUSTING OBEDIENCE

If we want God to reveal more of his will to us by his inspirations, we need to start by obeying his wishes that we already know. This obedience can be applied in various ways.

As we saw earlier, each act of faithfulness to grace attracts new graces, in ever-growing numbers. If we are attentive and obey the motions of the Holy Spirit, these graces will become more abundant. If we ignore inspirations, on the other hand, there is a danger that they will become less and less frequent. "To everyone who has more will be given; but from him who has not, even what he has will be taken away," [11] Jesus tells us. This is the beginning, then. To obtain more inspirations, we need to begin by obeying the ones we receive.

Next, it is obvious that God will grant us more inspirations if he sees us being faithful in fulfilling his will when it comes to us by other ways: the Commandments, the duties of our state in life, and so on. God's will is expressed in many ways, and we know these without any need for special inspirations. We know God's will as expressed in a general way through the commandments of Scripture, the teaching of the Church, the demands that are part

[11] Luke 19: 26.

of our vocation, and those that come from our job, for example.

If we have a sincere desire for faithfulness in these domains, God will favor us with more motions of his Spirit. If we are careless about our normal duties, then however much we beg God for special inspirations there is not much chance of his granting them.

Let's not forget either to consent, for love of God, to all the legitimate opportunities for obedience that present themselves in the areas of community, family, or social life. Of course we must obey God rather than men, but it would be an illusion to think we were capable of obeying God if we are incapable of obeying other people. The reason for this is that the same obstacle has to be overcome in both cases: attachment to ourselves and to our own will. If we can only obey people when it happens to please us, we are fooling ourselves about being able to obey the Holy Spirit. If we are never prepared to renounce our own will (our ideas, our tastes, our attachments) for other people, what guarantee is there that we'll be able to do so when God asks us to?

5. PRACTICE ABANDONMENT

Finally, we shouldn't forget the sort of obedience that may be the most important and the most overlooked: what might be called "obedience to events."

This notion obviously poses a difficult theological and existential problem. "Obedience to events" does not mean falling into fatalism or passivity, nor does it mean saying that everything that happens is God's will: God does not will evil or sin. Many things happen that God does not will. But he still permits them, in his wisdom, and they remain a stumbling block or scandal to our minds. God asks us to do all we can to eliminate evil. But despite our efforts, there is always a whole set of circumstances which we can do nothing about, which are not necessarily willed by God but nevertheless are permitted by him, and which God invites us to consent to trustingly and peacefully, even if they make us suffer and cause us problems. We are not being asked to consent to evil, but to consent to the mysterious wisdom of God who permits evil. Our consent is not a compromise with evil but the expression of our trust that God is stronger than evil. This is a form of obedience that is painful but very fruitful. It means that after we have done everything in our power, we are invited, faced with what is still imposed on our will by events, to practice an attitude of abandonment and filial trust toward our heavenly Father, in the faith that "for those who love God, everything works together for good." [12] To give an example, God did not want the treachery of Judas or Pilate's cowardice (God cannot want sin); but he permitted them, and he wanted Jesus to give filial consent to these events. And that is what he did—"Father, not what I will, but what thou wilt." [13]

[12] Romans 8: 28.
[13] Mark 14: 36.

The events of life are, after all, the surest expression of God's will, because there is no danger of our interpreting them subjectively. If God sees that we are docile to events, able to consent peacefully and lovingly to what life's happenings "impose" on us, in a spirit of filial trust and abandonment to his will, there can be no doubt that he will multiply personal expressions of his will for us through the action of his Spirit who speaks to our hearts.

If, however, we always rebel and tense ourselves against difficulties, that kind of defiance of God will make it difficult for the Holy Spirit to guide our lives.

What most prevents us from becoming saints is undoubtedly the difficulty we have in consenting fully to *everything* that happens to us, not, as we have seen, in the sense of a fatalistic passivity, but in the sense of a trusting total abandonment into the hands of our Father God.

What often happens is that, when we are confronted with painful occurrences, we either rebel, or endure them unwillingly, or resign ourselves to them passively.

But God invites us to a much more positive and fruitful attitude: that of St. Thérèse of Lisieux, who, as a child, said: "I choose it all!" We can give this the meaning: I choose everything that God wants for me. I won't content myself with merely enduring, but by a free act of my will; I *decide to choose what I have not chosen*. St. Thérèse used the expression: "I *want* everything that causes me difficulties." [14] Externally it doesn't change anything about the situation, but interiorly it changes everything. This consent, inspired by love and trust, makes us free and active instead of passive, and enables God to draw good out of everything that happens to us whether good or bad.

6. PRACTICE DETACHMENT

We cannot receive the motions of the Holy Spirit if we are rigidly attached to our possessions, our ideas, or our point of view. To allow ourselves to be led by the Spirit of God, we need great compliance and adaptability, and we can acquire these little by little by practicing detachment. We should make an effort not to "hang on to" anything, either materially, or affectively, or even spiritually. The detachment we should aim for is not that of saying "to hell with all of it," or of becoming indifferent to everything, or of practicing a sort of forced asceticism and stripping ourselves of everything that makes up our lives; that kind of detachment is not what our Lord normally asks for.

But we need to keep our hearts in an attitude of detachment, maintaining a sort of freedom, a distance, an inner reserve, that will mean that if some particular thing, or habit, or relationship, or personal plan is taken from us, we don't make a drama out of being deprived of it. Such detachment should be exercised in all aspects of our lives. But it is not the material aspect that is the most important.

---

[14] This expression is quoted by Sister Geneviève in *Conseils et Souvenirs*.

We are sometimes far more hampered in our spiritual progress by attachment to our own ideas, points of view, and ways of doing things.

We may find it profitable to read the advice of a sixteenth-century Franciscan:

> Let your will always be ready for anything that happens, and your affections perfectly disengaged. Want no one thing more than another; but if you do, let it be in such a manner that if not that thing, but the contrary were to happen, you would receive no upset but equal satisfaction. True liberty is to adhere to nothing, to have no dependence, no bias. God does not perform his wonders except in a thus solitary and disinterested soul.[15]

Even when the goals we are aiming at are excellent in themselves, attachment to our own "wisdom" may be a seriously bad obstacle in the way of docility to the Holy Spirit. Such an obstacle is all the greater in that this kind of attachment often goes unnoticed, because it is obviously easier to be unaware that we are attached to our own will when what we want is good in itself. Since the object we are aiming at is good, we feel justified in wanting it with a stubbornness that blinds us; and we don't realize that the way we want our idea to come about is not necessarily in accordance with God's plans.

[15] John de Bonilla, *Pax Animae* (Westminster, Md.: Newman Press, 1949), chap. 5.

Our wisdom and God's practically never coincide perfectly; and this lack of congruence means that at any stage of our spiritual journey, we shall never be dispensed from practicing detachment from our personal ideas, however well-intentioned these may be.

7. PRACTICE SILENCE AND PEACE

The Spirit of God is a spirit of peace, and he speaks and acts in peace and gentleness, never in tumult and agitation. What's more, the motions of the Spirit are delicate touches that don't make a great noise and can penetrate our spiritual consciousness only if we have within ourselves a sort of calm zone of silence and peace. If our inner world is noisy and agitated, the gentle voice of the Holy Spirit will find it very difficult to be heard.

If we want to recognize and follow the Spirit's motions, it is of the greatest importance to maintain a peaceful heart in all circumstances.

It isn't easy; but by practicing hope in God, abandonment, humility, and the acceptance of our inner poverty through an unshakeable trust in God's mercy, we will reach peace little by little. This theme has already formed the subject of another book[16] and so does not need to be repeated at length here. But it is important to underline the importance of peace of mind, because if we don't seek actively to "practice peace" in all the cir-

---

[16] Jacques Philippe, *Searching for and Maintaining Peace* (New York: Alba House, 2002).

cumstances that threaten to make us lose it (and there are plenty of them!) it will be difficult for us to hear the Holy Spirit's voice when he wants to speak—the agitation we allow in our hearts will almost certainly prevent it. As explained in the book mentioned above, when we experience difficult moments, the effort that we make to remain at peace in spite of everything does a lot of good, because the very fact of maintaining peace of mind will give us the best chance of reacting to the situation not in a human, agitated, hasty way (and making plenty of messes) but in a way that is attentive to what the Holy Spirit might suggest to us, which will obviously be much more profitable. So we should put into practice what St. John of the Cross said:

> Take care to preserve your heart in peace; let no happening of this world upset it. . . . Even if everything here below crumbled apart and all things were against us, there would be no use in upsetting ourselves over it, for that upset would bring us more harm than benefit.[17]

The greatest harm that upsetting ourselves does to us is that it makes us incapable of following the impulses of the Holy Spirit.

Maintaining peace is linked to the practice of silence. This silence is not an empty silence: it is peace, attentive-

[17] St. John of the Cross, Maxims 173 and 175.

ness to God's presence and attentiveness to others, waiting in trust and hope in God. We sometimes let ourselves be overtaken by excessive noise—not so much physical noise as the ceaseless whirlwind of thoughts, imaginations, and words that we've heard or said—and all this merely feeds our worries, fears, and frustrations, and obviously leaves the Holy Spirit little chance of making himself heard. Silence is not emptiness but that general attitude of inwardness that enables us to have an "inner cell" in our heart, to use an expression of St. Catherine of Siena's, where we are in God's presence and converse with him. Silence is the opposite of the dissipation of the soul in curiosity, gossip, and so forth. It is a capacity for returning almost spontaneously within ourselves, drawn by the presence of God within us.

8. PERSEVERE FAITHFULLY IN PRAYER

All of these attitudes, which facilitate the Holy Spirit's motions, can only be acquired little by little; and an absolute requirement for acquiring them is faithfulness to prayer. Prayer is indispensable in strengthening our determination to refuse God nothing, in practicing detachment with filial and trusting abandonment, in learning to love silence and inwardness, and in discovering the "place of the heart" where the Holy Spirit gently appeals to us. Again, as prayer has been the subject of a previous book[18]

[18] Jacques Philippe, *Time for God: A Guide to Prayer* (New York: Pauline Books and Media, 2005).

it will not be dealt with extensively here, but we need to remember how beneficial it is to dedicate time, regularly and faithfully, to the personal, silent prayer that Jesus himself recommends to us: "When you pray, go into your room and shut the door and pray to your Father who is in secret; and your Father who sees in secret will reward you." [19]

9. EXAMINE THE MOVEMENTS OF OUR HEARTS

Where are these inspirations of grace born? Not in our imagination or our head: they well up from the depths of our hearts. To recognize them, therefore, we need to pay attention to what is happening in our hearts, to the "movements" we can perceive there, and learn to discern when those movements come from our nature, from the action of the devil, or from the influence of the Holy Spirit. The question of how to learn this discernment will be discussed later on. But for the moment, this needs to be said: if we practice the advice given above, the outcome will be a capacity for attending to what happens within us at the deepest and most important level, which is not the level where there is most commotion, but is the intimate place of the heart that we become aware of little by little where the Holy Spirit brings his motions to birth in us.

It is by learning to take account of the various movements of our souls that we will learn to recognize the Holy

19 Matthew 6: 6.

Spirit's motions. This doesn't mean that we should fall into a kind of continual introspection: that would center us on ourselves or leave us at the mercy of our changing emotions and thoughts, and so produce no good at all. It means we should live in such a habitual disposition of desire for God, inner calm, prayer, and attentiveness to what is happening within us that, if a movement of grace is born in our hearts, it is not swamped or lost in the "background noise" of other things competing for our attention, but can emerge into our consciousness and be recognized as divine inspiration.

That recognition demands vigilance, leading us to examine from time to time what motivates us to do one thing rather than another. That sort of attentiveness will make us able to recognize various different movements within ourselves.

Some are "disordered" movements, that is, impulses to do or say something springing from an unhealthy origin. Often, for example, we are motivated by fear, resentment, anger, aggressiveness, the need to be noticed or admired by others, sensuality, and so on. These disordered motions may come from our "corrupt nature," as it used to be termed; today they would be said to come from our "wounds," which is the same thing. They may also come from the devil: these are temptations.

Sometimes, however, we are moved by good impulses: a sincere, disinterested desire to help someone else, and so on. These good movements can originate in our nature (not everything in us is totally corrupt!) or have a supernatural origin; in other words they may be the fruit of the work of God's grace in our hearts.

We should also realize that certain movements that are apparently good (because their object seems good) may not be so in reality, but may in fact come from the devil, who is cunning and sometimes impels us to do something that, although it appears good, would be contrary to God's will for us and would produce harmful results in our lives.

The climate of inwardness described above helps us to realize the different character of these movements, their origins, and their effects: for example, those that leave joy and peace in our hearts, and those that do the opposite, stirring up anxiety and sadness.

This examination of our hearts especially will help us to realize certain movements that arise in us from time to time, and that with a little experience we can learn to identify as invitations from the Holy Spirit to do (or not do) certain things. These are the inspirations of grace that were mentioned earlier and that are so important to be able to follow, because they are very fruitful for our spiritual progress and extremely valuable in helping us in our service to God and our neighbor. There may be many or few of them—that is up to God. But the fewer of them we miss, the better, because they open us up to the action of the Spirit, who "helps us in our weakness." [20]

[20] Romans 8: 26.

10. OPEN OUR HEARTS TO A SPIRITUAL DIRECTOR

We will find it much easier to discern the action of the Holy Spirit if we have the possibility of opening our hearts to someone who can give us spiritual guidance. Very often we cannot see clearly into ourselves, or discern our motivations, and light will come when we put what we are living through into words, talking to someone experienced in the spiritual life.

We need to know that this opening of our hearts is something God blesses. The reason is that it shows humility—we acknowledge that we are not sufficient of ourselves. It also shows trust in the other person, and it shows a sincere desire to see clearly in order to do God's will because we are doing something about it. These dispositions are very pleasing to God, and he never fails to reward them with his graces. We therefore should pray as hard as we can to our Lord to give us someone we can open our hearts to, and should make use of the opportunities he offers us to that end; these acts sometimes take quite a bit of courage. However, we should not despair if, through no fault of our own, this does not happen often. If we sincerely desire a spiritual director but cannot find one, God will provide otherwise.

Finally, frequent Confession should never be neglected, even if it does not lead to spiritual direction, because it is a source of purification of the heart and gives light to understand the things that happen in our souls.

III

HOW CAN WE KNOW THAT AN INSPIRATION COMES FROM GOD?

We now come to the most delicate question. In the sometimes confused crowd of thoughts, emotions, and feelings inside us, how can we recognize the inspirations that have God as their origin? How can we identify what comes from the Holy Spirit, and not confuse it with what may be the fruit of our imagination, wishful thinking, or temptations from the devil?

Obviously there are no ready-made answers. Our self and the various influences it is subject to, whether psychological or spiritual, is such a complex domain that it is impossible for us to reduce the discernment of the motions of the Holy Spirit to a few rules of thumb.

However, there are certain remarks and criteria that can help to orient us here. They cannot provide a way of discerning with certainty because there is no hard-and-fast certainty to be had on this question, but they are sufficient to point the way forward (more as though feeling our way rather than seeing) and to enable us to cooperate more and more closely with God's grace.

I. PROGRESSIVELY ACQUIRE A "SPIRITUAL SENSE"

Before going over the criteria that enable us to discern the motions of the Holy Spirit, there is one important point to emphasize here. Ultimately what will help us to recognize and respond to God's motions most easily and promptly is the interior development of a sort of "spiritual sense," which to begin with we may not have at all or may have only in a very rough form. We can develop this sense by experience, and especially by faithfully and resolutely following our Lord.[1]

This "spiritual hearing" is a kind of ability to recognize, among all the multiple, discordant voices that we can hear inside us, the unique, unmistakable voice of Jesus. This sense is like a loving instinct that makes it easier and easier for us to distinguish the voice of the Spouse, in the chorus of sounds that greet our ears.

The Holy Spirit uses, for each of us, a "tone of voice" that is his alone. It has particular gentleness and power, purity and clarity, which, when we are accustomed to hearing it, gives us near-certainty in singling it out. Of course, the devil, aping what he can of God's ways, can

---

[1] The development of this "spiritual sense" draws on the theology of the "gifts of the Holy Spirit" as expounded by St. Thomas Aquinas and many other saints, each in his own way. In order to keep the present book as simple as possible, a detailed discussion of the various gifts of the Holy Spirit will not be given here. See, however, Appendix 3: Quotations from St. Francis de Sales.

sometimes try to imitate the voice of the Spouse. But if we are truly accustomed to the voice of the Spirit by loving familiarity and by a constant, pure seeking after God's will, we will easily distinguish the voice that, even if it's a good imitation, sounds wrong in some way and so is not the voice of Jesus.

In St. John's Gospel Jesus promises us that the Holy Spirit will give this spiritual sense to us progressively. Speaking of himself as the Good Shepherd, he says: "The sheep follow him, for they know his voice. They will not follow a stranger, but will flee from him, for they do not know the voice of strangers." [2]

2. CRITERIA CONFIRMING THAT AN INSPIRATION COMES FROM GOD

To take shape in us, this spiritual sense needs to be based on sound methods of judging and discerning. The principal ones are the following.

External criterion: God doesn't contradict Himself

There are a certain number of criteria that one could term "external," which inspirations must match if they come from God; these criteria mainly enable us to eliminate certain pseudo-inspirations that present them-

[2] John 10: 4–5.

46

selves. These criteria are a necessary result of God's self-consistency. The Holy Spirit cannot, in his inspirations, ask us for anything that contradicts his will as expressed by the more usual means: the Word of God, the teaching of the Church, and the demands of our vocation.

Consistency with Holy Scripture and the teaching of the Church

A divine inspiration cannot ask us to do something that contradicts what the Word of God teaches and asks of us. This means not the Word of God as compiled by each individual's fantasy and interpretation, but Holy Scripture as transmitted and explained by the teaching authority of the Church. For example, a divine inspiration cannot ask me to commit acts that the Church considers immoral.

In the same way, true inspirations always go in the direction of a spirit of obedience to the Church. A religious who disobeyed his superiors, or a bishop who disobeyed the Holy Father, even for a purpose that was praiseworthy in itself, definitely would not be acting under divine inspiration. "When God puts inspirations into a heart, the first he gives is obedience,"[3] says St. Francis de Sales.

---

[3] St. Francis de Sales, *Treatise on the Love of God*, book 8, chap. 13 (p. 360 of the Mackey translation).

Consistency with the demands of our vocation

A whole collection of demands are derived from our own vocation as a married person, a parent, a priest, a religious, et cetera, and from our situation in life (our professional duties, etc.); and these demands are God's will for us. An inspiration, if it comes from God, cannot ask us for something that is in manifest contradiction to what used to be called our "duties of state." The Holy Spirit may encourage a mother to be somewhat less occupied with her household cares so that she can dedicate some time to prayer. But if he suggested to her that she should spend so much time in contemplation that her husband and children suffered, there would be good reason to question the source of this inspiration. Inspirations go in the same direction as our duties of state and do not divert us from them but, just the reverse, help us to fulfill them.

The application of this criterion may sometimes be a little delicate. The limits of our duties of state are not necessarily clear-cut, and a contradiction between them and certain divine inspirations may be more apparent than real. The history of the Church includes some extreme examples in this area: there was St. Nicholas of Flüe who abandoned his family, or St. Jane Frances de Chantal who stepped over one of her sons where he was sleeping in a doorway to prevent her from following her call to found the Visitation Order. But these decisions were not sudden impulses; they had matured for a long time in prayer and reflection, and submitted to the discernment of a spiritual director.

It sometimes happens that we make our family or professional duties into a comfortable excuse for not doing what the Holy Spirit asks. But it remains true that this criterion of consistency between divine inspirations and the demands of our state in life is an important one, and we could avoid many spiritual illusions simply by taking it into account.

Internal criterion: A tree is known by its fruit

The most important criterion for discerning divine inspirations is the one that Jesus himself gives us in the Gospel: "A tree is known by its fruit." An inspiration from God, if we follow it, will produce sound fruit: the fruits of peace, joy, charity, communion, and humility. An inspiration that comes from our flesh or from the devil will be sterile or even bear the negative fruits of sadness, bitterness, pride, and the like.

This criterion is an important one, but its big disadvantage is that it can only be applied in retrospect. Once it has been followed its consequences can be measured. But in practice we would obviously prefer to have some means of judging that would enable us to forestall mistakes, to know whether an inspiration came from God or not before putting it into effect!

49

Despite its disadvantage, this criterion is not at all useless. First, it lets us gain experience. And secondly, even before putting the decision into effect, certain fruits may already make themselves apparent within us—the fruits of peace, joy, and so on.

Building up our experience

As stated above, our ability to recognize the motions of the Holy Spirit stems from the acquisition of a kind of "spiritual sense." This spiritual sense is a gift from God, but it is developed and strengthened by experience, too.

When we see the results produced by decisions we took following what we thought were inspirations, we very often shall be able to tell whether in fact our "idea" came from God or whether it was a product of our own minds alone. That won't always be pleasant for our pride; we don't particularly like admitting that we were mistaken. But we have to go through that experience.

We need to know that in the spiritual life, even if we are full of good will, and can be sure that God helps us with great faithfulness, we are never dispensed from a learning process, which involves trial and error, successes and failures. God wants things to be that way; it is a human law that nobody, not even the most spiritual person in the world, is exempt from. If we learn the lessons of experience humbly and go forward without getting discouraged, trusting that "all is grace," then we will build up greater certainty of judgment. This certainty will never become infallible, because the only infallibility that exists in this world is the charism possessed by the Pope, and the Ecumenical Councils in communion with him, when he defines *ex cathedra* a matter concerning faith or morals to be held by the whole Church.

However, the experience of objective results, the confirmations or refutations provided by facts, and also the inner state we are left with by our decisions (the fact of whether they leave us peaceful, humble, and joyful, or sad, upset, and tense) will all help us to learn how to recognize what comes from God and distinguish it from what comes from the devil or from ourselves, our character traits, tendencies, and so forth.

Discernment of spirits

The experience of the Church and the saints[4] demonstrates a general law: what comes from the Spirit of God brings with it joy, peace, tranquility of spirit, gentleness, simplicity, and light. On the other hand, what comes from the spirit of evil brings sadness, trouble, agitation, worry, confusion, and darkness. These marks of the good and the evil spirit are unmistakable signs in themselves. Peace, joy, and the like are certain fruits of the Holy Spirit; the devil is incapable of producing them in a

[4] See, for example, St. Ignatius of Loyola, *Spiritual Exercises*, chapter on the discernment of spirits.

lasting way. And since, by contrast, trouble and sadness are the sure marks of the evil spirit, the Holy Spirit cannot be the source of them.

There is, of course, the "sadness that leads to repentance," which is caused by the Holy Spirit. But if it really does lead us to repent, it quickly turns into joy. Moreover, that sadness does not itself actually come from the Holy Spirit, only insofar as the Holy Spirit has brought to light something within us that is wrong and needs to be made right. Out of all the marks of the good and evil spirit, the most characteristic of all is peace. The Spirit of God unfailingly produces peace in our souls, and the devil unfailingly produces agitation.

In practice, however, things are more complex. An inspiration may come from God and still cause a lot of turbulence in us. But this turbulence does not come from the inspiration, which in itself (like everything that comes from the Spirit of God) is gentle and peaceable. The turbulence comes from our resistance to that inspiration. Once we accept the inspiration and cease to put up resistance to it, then our heart finds itself settled in deep peace.

This situation happens frequently. Certain inspirations of grace, when they reach us, meet with resistance from us, whether or not we are aware of it, and they arouse fear on the human plane, come up against our attachments to our own habits and the like. The idea of putting what the Holy Spirit is suggesting into practice worries us, and we start thinking: "How can I? What are other people going to think about me? Do I have the strength to do it?" and so on.

To describe this situation, we can use the image of a great river flowing tranquilly which produces eddies and whirlpools when it meets obstacles.

If an inspiration truly comes from God, and we silence our fears and consent to it wholeheartedly, in the end we shall be filled with irresistible peace; for the Holy Spirit will not fail to produce such peace in those who allow themselves to be led by him. This peace sometimes dwells only in the very deepest part of the soul, while questions and worries remain at the human and psychological level, but it is there and it is recognizable.

By contrast, if an inspiration comes from the devil or from our own ambitious, selfishness, exaggerated need for being recognized by others, and so forth, and we consent to it, it can never leave our heart in total, deep peace. Any peace it does bring will only be superficial, and will soon disappear, to be replaced by disturbance. We may refuse to acknowledge this disturbance and relegate it to the depths of our minds, but it is still there, ready to re-emerge at the moment of truth.

We need to note this important point: *A divine inspiration can disturb us to begin with, but to the extent that we do not refuse it, but open ourselves to it and consent to it, little by little it will establish peace in us.*

That is a fundamental law, which applies in the "normal" situations of the spiritual life, and for those who are sincerely disposed to do God's will in everything. However, the spiritual life and the interaction between the spiritual and psychological elements are complex, and so there may sometimes be trying situations, or particular temperaments, that make it difficult to apply this criterion in practice. But it is still a basic one and is found throughout the tradition of the Church.

Complementary signs: Constancy and humility

One of the characteristics of God's Spirit is constancy. And by contrast what comes from our flesh or the evil spirit is unstable and changing. There is nothing more inconstant than our moods and wishes, as we know. The same is true of the devil: he pushes us in one direction, then another, distracts us from one project to take up a new one, so that in the end nothing gets done at all. One of the strategies he often uses to stop us from accomplishing a good project is to paint a different one in glowing colors, to distract us from the first one.

Divine inspirations, on the other hand, are stable and constant. For that reason it is a good general rule not to be overly hasty in following an inspiration (especially, of course, in a really important matter), in order to verify that it doesn't soon vanish completely; such evaporation could be a sign that it was not from God.

Another characteristic of God's Spirit is that, while enlightening us and impelling us to act, he imprints our souls with a deep sense of humility. He makes us do good in such a way that we are happy to do it, but without any presumptuousness, self-satisfaction, or vanity. We see quite clearly that the good that we do does not come from ourselves but from God.

When we are moved by the Holy Spirit, there may well be (because we are human) some little thought of vainglory that starts to grow in us like a parasite (and that we should fight against), but deep down we see very clearly that we are only weak, that all the good we can do comes from God, and that we have precisely nothing to boast about. This true humility is absent from those who are acting under the impulse of their own flesh or the devil. And, let's not forget, one of the surest tests of true humility is the spirit of obedience.

To sum up, we could say that divine inspirations are recognizable by this: they establish us in peace, are not changeable, and impress on us a sense of humility.

Some further remarks on the subject of discerning divine inspirations will be useful at this point.

Is God's will always the choice that is most difficult?

God's will, and hence the inspirations of his grace, obviously often go in the opposite direction from our immediate tendencies, in the sense that our tendency is often toward the desire for selfish comfort, ease, laziness, and so on. St. John of the Cross tells us, in a celebrated passage:

"Let the soul apply itself ceaselessly not to what is easiest, but to what is most difficult . . ., not to what pleases, but to what displeases." [5]

He is not wrong to say this, in that context. But we should not interpret his maxims wrongly, or take as a systematic rule for discerning God's will the principle that in any given situation what he asks of us will always be what is most difficult. That would make us fall into an exaggerated ascetical voluntarism that had nothing to do with the freedom of the Holy Spirit. We might even add that the idea that God is always asking us for what we find most difficult is the kind of thought that the devil typically suggests in order to discourage people and turn them away from God.

God is a Father, and he is certainly a demanding one because he loves us and invites us to give him everything; but he is not an executioner. He very often leaves us to our free choice. When he requires something of us, it is to help us grow in love. The only commandment is to love. We can suffer for love, but we can also rejoice in love and rest in love. It is a trap of our imagination or of the devil to picture a life spent following God as something imprisoning, in complete, constant contradiction with all our own desires, even the most legitimate ones.

God's aim is not to complicate our lives, but ultimately to make them simpler. Docility to God sets our hearts free

---

[5] St. John of the Cross, *Ascent of Mount Carmel*, book 1, chap. 13.

and expands them. This is why Jesus, who invites us to renounce ourselves and take up our crosses to follow him, also tells us: "My yoke is easy, and my burden is light." [6] Even if we sometimes find it difficult to do God's will, especially at the start, if we do it lovingly we end up filled with joy; and it's true to say it is a real pleasure to do the good that God inspires in us. The more we journey in docility to the Holy Spirit, the less painful and forced, the freer and more spontaneous, our adherence to God's will becomes. "Lead me in the path of thy commandments, for I delight in it," [7] says the Psalmist.

It's true that life is made of trials; but if we are constantly sad and discontented in a certain path, we would have to question seriously whether we were on the right route, or if we were not actually in the process of imposing burdens on ourselves that God is not asking of us. One of the criteria for discerning a vocation is whether the person is happy in it. To imagine, as certain scrupulous or falsely ascetical people do, that what God requires of us in every circumstance is necessarily the most difficult thing, can seriously deform our judgment; and the devil can make use of this false idea to deceive us. And so bear this in mind.

I want to tell you something. Sometimes, after a tiring day, happy to be getting to bed at last, I perceive a little inner feeling that says to me, "Won't you come to the

[6] Matthew 11: 30.
[7] Psalm 119: 35.

chapel to keep me company for a moment?" After a few seconds of fighting back and resisting, saying things like "Jesus, you're exaggerating. I'm tired, and if I don't get enough sleep I'll be in a bad mood tomorrow!" I finally consent and spend a few minutes with Jesus. After that I go to bed in peace, very happy; and the following day I'm no more tired than usual when I get up. Thank you, Lord—that is certainly your will: the fruits are there to see.

But sometimes the opposite happens. I may have a big problem worrying me, and tell myself: "This evening I'm going to pray for this to be sorted out." As I go toward the chapel for this purpose, a little voice says in my heart: "You know, you'd give me more pleasure by going straight to bed and trusting me; I'll take care of your problem." And, recalling my happy situation as a "useless servant," I go to bed in peace, abandoning everything into our Lord's hands . . .

All that is just to say that God's will is where there is the maximum of love, but not necessarily where there is the maximum of suffering. There is more love in resting in trust than making ourselves suffer through worrying!

Different reactions depending on the importance of the inspirations

To know how to react to what we think are divine inspirations, we also need to take into account an aspect that has not yet been discussed: the object of these inspirations and their relative importance.

The Lord may inspire us to distribute all our possessions to the poor and go off to live in the desert, imitating St. Anthony the Great, and he may inspire us about the very smallest things, as in the examples just given.

Now, as has already been said, it is very important to do our best not to neglect a single one of God's inspirations. Something that seems insignificant to us may be more important than we imagine. I remember how one day, when I was preaching a retreat, I struggled hard against obeying an inner motion suggesting that I should invite the participants, while saying a rosary, to venerate a cross that had been set up and garlanded with flowers by some children. I told myself, "It'll take too long; it isn't the right moment for it," and so on. After I acquiesced, in the course of the act of veneration, one of the people there was cured of a serious spinal problem.

Moreover, one small act of obedience to God can sometimes cause us to make more progress spiritually than years of effort according to our own plans. Fidelity to small graces draws down bigger ones.

That being said, it is also obvious that we should treat inspirations differently depending on their importance. As St. Francis de Sales said, you don't count small change in the same way as you count gold ingots.[8] The latter

---

[8] See the text in Appendix 3.

have to be weighed carefully and accurately, whereas for the former, it would be foolish to spend an undue amount of time and care on it.

Let's notice in passing that many of the Spirit's motions do not, in a sense, need any deliberation at all: it's often a question of an inner movement that helps us to do something that we ought to do in any case. For instance, maybe we're feeling bitter against someone, and we feel moved to forgive them. Or, it's time to go to Mass and we are tempted to carry on working on an urgent job, which is going to make us arrive late; and we feel a motion that impels us to leave everything as it is and go to Mass. All we have to do is follow those movements, since they are clearly good ones. Just as the devil tempts us, so too the Holy Spirit, in the opposite sense, appeals to us, stirs us up, and awakens us interiorly to make it easer for us to do what God desires of us. And unquestionably he would do this still more often if we were more attentive and obedient to his motions. Here is what St. Francis de Sales says: [9]

> Without inspiration our souls would lead an idle, sluggish, and fruitless life, but on receiving the divine rays of inspiration we are sensible of a light mingled with a quickening heat, which illuminates our understanding, and which excites and ani-

[9] St. Francis de Sales, *Treatise on the Love of God*, book 8, chap. 10 (pp. 349–350 of the Mackey translation).

mates our will, giving it the strength to will and effect the good which is necessary for eternal salvation.

Sometimes a suggestion comes to us to do something unusual, which does not form part of our normal round of activities, but is not enormously important. Some examples of this have already been considered. Our Lord impels us to an act of charity, a deed of service, a moment of prayer, a little sacrifice, an act of humility, and so on. In such cases we should make a rapid evaluation of the idea. If it seems reasonable, compatible with our obligations, if (according to our experience of God's methods of teaching us) we think we really can recognize Jesus' voice, and if, finally, the more we consent to it the more we feel at peace, then all we have to do is put it into practice. If we are wrong, and realize afterwards that it was really a movement of vainglory, presumptuousness, or an idea of our own, then there's no great harm done, and it will be useful for our spiritual education. And God our Lord won't hold it against us.

However, when the suggestion that comes to us is about much more important things—a vocation, a change of direction in our life, choices that may have serious repercussions on other people, or else something that clearly goes beyond the habitual rule of life for the vocation we have received—then it is essential not to decide anything without submitting that inspiration to a spiritual director or a superior. This act of obedience pleases God, even if it may sometimes apparently slow down the fulfillment of the thing that he himself is asking us to do. God prefers that prudence and submission on our part, to undue precipitation.

Without that obedience, by contrast, it is very probable that we will soon become the plaything of the devil who, seeing how quick we are to follow inspirations without submitting them, when necessary, to obedience, will lose no time in deceiving us and leading us little by little to do things that no longer have anything to do with the will of God.

In case of doubt on what line of conduct to follow, it is normally best to open our hearts to one or more than one person and to follow their advice (unless there is a decisive reason for acting otherwise), rather than spend a long time reflecting and weighing things up personally, which might cause us to go round in circles and increase our confusion rather than diminishing it.

Being unresponsive to grace

We have seen how important it is not to neglect or ignore any of God's inspirations. This may make us fear that our unfaithfulness to those inspirations may have harmed our relationship with our Lord beyond repair.

But the reason for stressing the point is to raise our awareness of the importance of cooperating with God and what he wants to do in our lives, and make us more attentive to him; not to arouse a fear that will worry and discourage us. We should do all we can to avoid being unfaithful to him, but at the same time we should believe that when we fail, it is by no means irremediable.

Our Lord is always ready to lift us up again when we fall, and he even finds a way to make our falls beneficial to us if after them we turn back to him with a humble, trusting heart. Every time we realize that through superficiality, carelessness, or cowardice we have stifled or ignored some inspiration, let's not be discouraged by it. Let's sincerely ask our Lord to forgive us, take occasion of it to humble ourselves and recognize how short of virtue we are, and ask him to "punish" us by granting us an extra measure of faithfulness so that we can make up for all the graces we lost!

For God, that is not at all impossible—if we expect it of him with the daring trust of children, he will grant it to us.

CONCLUSION

We have looked at some of the conditions for enabling God's inspirations to make themselves felt in our lives and become more frequent, so that we can be progressively guided and moved by the Holy Spirit.

The conditions listed above would be incomplete without one final addition. This condition is filial love for our Lady. Out of all created beings, the Virgin Mary is the one who most lived in the shadow of the Holy Spirit.[1] Mary's whole life was a perfect act of consent to all the operations of the Spirit in her, and this led her to a more and more ardent and ever higher degree of love. Appendix 3 gives a beautiful text from the writings of St. Francis de Sales that can help us to understand how Mary's love grew steadily because the Holy Spirit met with no resistance in her.

Mary is our mother in the order of grace. As such, she hands on to us the fullness of grace that is hers. And I think that of all the gifts that Mary grants to those who recognize themselves as her children, and who "take her into their own homes" following the example of the beloved disciple St. John,[2] the most precious is a share in her total availability to grace, her capacity to let herself

[1] See Luke 1: 35: "The Holy Spirit will come upon you, and the power of the Most High will overshadow you."
[2] See John 19: 27.

65

be led by the Holy Spirit without resisting. Mary passes on to us her humility, her trust in God, her total self-giving to God's will, her silence, and her inner listening to the Spirit. This means that one of the surest ways by which we will little by little become able to put into practice the indications contained in this book is to entrust the whole of our spiritual life to our Lady. She will teach us what she practiced so well: to recognize clearly, to receive with full trust, and to put into practice with total fidelity, all the suggestions of grace by which God will work marvels of love in our lives, as he did in the life of his humble handmaid.

APPENDICES

A Prayer by Cardinal Mercier

I am going to show you a secret about holiness and happiness. For five minutes every day let your imagination be quiet, close your eyes to everything they see, and shut your ears to of all the world's noise so that you can withdraw into the sanctuary of your baptized soul, the temple of the Holy Ghost. And speak to that holy spirit and say to Him:

> *Holy Spirit, soul of my soul, I adore Thee.*
> *Enlighten me, guide me,*
> *strengthen and comfort me.*
> *Tell me what I ought to do*
> *and order me to do it.*
> *I promise to submit*
> *to anything that you requirest from me,*
> *and to accept everything*
> *that Thou allowest to happen to me.*
> *Just show me what Thy will is.*

If you do this your life will be quiet and peaceful, and comfort will abound even in the middle of troubles. For grace will be given to match any stress together with strength to bear it, grace that will take you to the gates of Paradise, full of merit. Such submission to the Holy Spirit is the secret of holiness. «

Appendix II

Quotations from Fr. Louis Lallemant (1587–1635)

Father Lallemant was one of the great figures in the Society of Jesus in seventeenth-century France. He was in charge of the "Third Year," the last year of training in Jesuit formation; and among his students were saints such as Isaac Jogues and Jean de Brébeuf, who were martyred in North America. At the heart of his spiritual teaching he placed docility to the Holy Spirit, together with the purification of the heart or practice of detachment that makes such docility possible. Notes taken from the conferences he gave have been collected into a book,[1] and the following passages are extracts from it.

1. *Docility to the Holy Spirit*

When souls have abandoned themselves to be led by the Holy Spirit he raises them little by little and guides them. At the beginning these souls do not know where they are being led, but little by little a light shines within and makes them see all their actions and the guidance of God on their actions, so that they have almost nothing else to do than let God do whatever he chooses in them and through them; so that these souls advance marvelously.

[1] Louis Lallemant, *Doctrine spirituelle* (Bruges: Desclée de Brouwer, 1959); English ed.: *The Spiritual Doctrine of Father Louis Lallemant* (Westminster, Md.: Newman Book Shop, 1946).

70

We have a figure of the guidance of the Holy Spirit in God's guidance of the Israelites after their escape from Egypt, as they journeyed through the desert to reach the Promised Land. He guided them with a pillar of cloud by day and of fire by night. They followed the movement of this pillar, and stopped when it stopped; they never overtook it but only followed it, and never separated themselves from it. That is how we should act toward the Holy Spirit.

2. *Means for reaching docility*

The main means for achieving this guidance of the Holy Spirit are:

1. Faithfully obeying God's wishes as far as we know them. There are many that we do not know, for we are all full of ignorance; but God will only call us to account for the things he has given us to know. If we make good use of these, he will give us more. If we accomplish what he has already made known to us of his designs, he will then show us the rest.

2. Frequently renew the good resolution to follow God's will in all things, and strengthen that resolution as much as we can.

3. Ask the Holy Spirit unceasingly for the light and strength to accomplish God's will; bind ourselves to the Holy Spirit and hold fast to him, like St. Paul, who said to the elders at Ephesus: "I am going to Jerusalem,

bound in the Spirit." [1] Especially on undertaking the most important activities, ask God for the light of the Holy Spirit, and tell him earnestly that we do not wish anything except to do his will. After which, if he does not give us any new lights, we will do, as we did up to that point, what we have been accustomed to do and what seems to us to be best.

4. Take careful note of the different movements of our soul. Through that diligence little by little we shall come to recognize what comes from God and what does not. What comes from God, in a soul subject to grace, is ordinarily peaceful and tranquil. What comes from the devil is violent, and brings trouble and anxiety with it.

3. *Response to certain objections to docility*

. . . The second objection is that it seems this inner guidance of the Holy Spirit destroys the obedience that is due to our superiors. The first reply to this objection is that, just as the inner inspiration of grace does not destroy the belief we give to the external proposition of the articles of faith, but rather gently inclines our understanding to believe, in the same way being led by the gifts of the Holy Spirit, far from diverting us from obedience, helps us to obey and makes obedience easier. Secondly, all that inner guidance, and even divine revelations, should

---

[1] Acts 20: 22.

always be subordinated to obedience, and should be heeded on the tacit condition that obedience does not order otherwise.

. . . The third objection is that this inner guiding by the Holy Spirit seems to render deliberation and consultation pointless. Why ask the opinion of men when we are guided by the Holy Spirit? The answer is that the Holy Spirit leads us to consult people who are enlightened, and follow advice. Thus he sent St. Paul to Ananias, to learn from him what he was to do.

. . . The fourth objection is from some who complain that they do not have guidance by the Spirit, and cannot recognize it.

The answer to these people is that the Holy Spirit's lights and inspirations, which are necessary for doing good and avoiding evil, are never lacking, especially if they are in the state of grace. Secondly, that, living on the outside as they do, hardly ever entering into themselves, examining their consciences very superficially, seeing only what is external and the faults that are apparent to the eyes of the world, without seeking the hidden roots, their passions and predominant habits, without examining the state and dispositions of their souls and the movements of their hearts, it is no wonder that they do not recognize the guidance of the Holy Spirit, who is entirely within us. How could they recognize him? They do not even know their inner sins, which are their own acts that they produce freely. But they will unfailingly come to know the guidance of the Holy Spirit if they take the trouble to develop the necessary dispositions.

Firstly, they need to follow faithfully the light that is given them: then it will grow steadily.

Secondly, they should cut back the sins and imperfections that, like so many clouds, rob them of that light: they will see more clearly day by day.

Thirdly, they should never allow their external senses to go astray and be dirtied by sensuality: then God will open the senses of their souls.

Fourthly, if possible they should never go out of their inner selves, or else should return as soon as possible; and they should be attentive to what takes place there. Then they will notice the movements of the different spirits that cause us to act.

Fifthly, they should sincerely reveal the whole depth of their hearts to their superior or spiritual director: a soul that possesses this candor and simplicity will never fail to be favored with the guidance of the Holy Spirit.

4. *Motives for docility: Perfection and even salvation depend on docility to grace*

1. The two elements of the spiritual life are the purification of the heart and the guidance of the Holy Spirit. Those are the two poles of the whole spiritual life. By these two ways we reach perfection according to the degree of purity we have acquired, and in proportion to

the fidelity we have shown in cooperating with the movements of the Holy Spirit and following his guidance.

All of our perfection depends on this fidelity; and the whole spiritual life could be summed up as taking note of the ways and movements of the Holy Spirit in our souls and strengthening our wills in the resolution to follow them, using for that purpose all the exercises of prayer, reading, the Sacraments, the practice of virtue, and the accomplishing of good works.

2. Some people have many beautiful practices and do a number of external acts of virtue; they place their effort in material acts of virtue. That is good for beginners, but it is much closer to perfection to follow the inner leading of the Holy Spirit and to be guided by his movements. It is true that in this latter way of acting there is less perceptible satisfaction, but there is more inner life and more real virtue.

3. The goal which we should aspire to, after we have exercised the purification of our hearts for a long time, is to be so possessed and governed by the Holy Spirit that it is he alone who leads all of our faculties and senses and who rules our interior and external movements, and that we abandon ourselves entirely by spiritual renunciation of our preferences and our own satisfactions. Thus we will no longer live in ourselves but in Jesus Christ, through full faithful response to the operations of his divine Spirit, and by perfect subjection of all our rebelliousness to the power of his grace. . . .

6. Our greatest evil is the opposition we present toward God's designs, and the resistance we make to his inspirations; for either we choose not to hear them, or having heard them we reject them, or having received them we weaken and dirty them by a thousand imperfections of attachment, complacency, and self-satisfaction.

However, the main point of spiritual life consists in so disposing ourselves to grace through purity of heart that, of two people who consecrate themselves at the same time to God's service, if one gives himself wholly to good works and the other applies himself entirely to purifying his heart and cutting away what there is in it that opposes grace, this second person will achieve perfection twice as quickly as the first.

Thus our greatest concern should be not so much to read spiritual books as to pay great attention to divine inspirations, which are sufficient with very little reading, and to be extremely faithful in corresponding to the graces that are offered to us.

7. It sometimes happens that having received a good inspiration from God, we soon find ourselves attacked by repugnance, doubts, bewilderment, and difficulties that come from our corrupt nature and from our passions that are contrary to divine inspiration. If we receive that inspiration with total submission of heart, it will fill us with the peace and consolation that the Spirit of God brings with him, and that he communicates to souls whom he encounters no resistance in.

5. *The excellence of grace, and the injustice of opposing it*

1. We ought to receive each inspiration as a word of God, which proceeds from his wisdom, his mercy, and his infinite goodness, and which can produce marvelous effects in us if we place no obstacle in its way. Let us consider what God's word has wrought: it created the heavens and the earth, and drew all creatures out of nothing to share in the being of God in the state of nature, because it met with no resistance in that nothingness. It would work something still greater in us if we did not resist it. It would draw us out of moral nothingness into a supernatural participation in the holiness of God in the state of grace, and to participation in the happiness of God in the state of glory. And for a little point of honor, for an occupation that satisfied our vanity, for a mere pleasure of a moment, for a trifle, we are willing to prevent these great effects from being wrought by God's word, his inspirations, and the impressions of his Spirit: after that, would you not admit that Wisdom was right in saying that the number of fools is infinite? [2]

2. If we could see the ways in which God's inspirations are received in our souls, we would see that they remain, so to speak, on the surface, without entering further in, since the opposition that they encounter in us prevents

---

[2] Ecclesiastes 1: 15 (Douai version).

them from making any impression; this happens because we do not give ourselves enough to the Spirit, and we do not serve God with sufficient fullness of heart. Thus, in order that graces have their effect in the hearts of sinners they have to enter with noise and violence, because they meet great resistance; but they penetrate gently into souls possessed by God, filling them with the admirable peace that always accompanies God's Spirit. And by contrast the suggestions of the enemy make no impression on good souls, because they find them ruled by opposing principles. «

Quotations from St. Francis de Sales (1567–1622)[1]

1. *Criteria for the discernment of spirits*

One of the best signs of the goodness of inspirations in general, and particularly of extraordinary ones, is peace and tranquility in the heart that receives them: for though indeed the Holy Spirit is violent, yet his violence is gentle, sweet, and peaceful. He comes as a *mighty wind* [Acts 2:2] and as heavenly thunder, but he does not knock the Apostles down, he does not upset them; the fear they had in hearing the sound was momentary, and was immediately followed by sweet assurance . . .

On the contrary, the evil spirit is turbulent, rough, disturbing; and those who follow infernal suggestions, thinking that they are heavenly inspirations, as a rule are easily identified, because they are loud, headstrong, proud, ready to undertake or meddle in all kinds of business, men who under the pretext of zeal turn everything upside down, censure everyone, scold everyone, find fault with everything; they are people who will not be directed, will not give in to anyone, will not put up with anything, but gratify the passions of self-love under the name of concern for God's honor [book 8, chap. 12].

[1] These texts are taken from the Mackey translation of the *Treatise on the Love of God*.

2. *Obedience, sign of the truth of inspirations*

Within obedience everything is secure; outside of it every-thing is suspect. When God puts inspirations in a heart, the first he gives is obedience. . . . Whoever says he is inspired, and still refuses to obey his superiors and follow their advice, is an impostor. The prophets and preachers that were inspired by God always loved the Church, always adhered to her doctrine, always were approved by her. . . . St. Francis, St. Dominic, and the other fathers of religious orders, were called to the service of souls by extraordinary inspiration, but they the more humbly and heartily submitted themselves to the sacred hierarchy of the Church. In conclusion, the three best and most assured marks of lawful inspirations are perseverance, against instability and casualness; peace and gentleness of heart, against worry and anxiety; humble obedience, against stubbornness and extravagance [book 8, chap. 13].

3. *Brief method of recognizing God's will*

St. Basil says that God's will is made clear to us by his ordinances or commandments, and that then there is no argument to be made, for we simply are to do what is ordained; but that for other things we have freedom to choose what seems good according to our liking though we are not to do everything that is allowable but only what is advisable, and to discern clearly what is advisable we are to follow the advice of our spiritual father.

But, Theotimus, I warn you about a troublesome temptation which often comes to souls who have a great desire to do what is closest to God's will. For the enemy at every choice makes them doubt whether it is God's will for them to do one thing rather than another; as for example, whether they should eat with a friend or not, whether they should wear gray or black clothes, whether they should fast Friday or Saturday, whether they should enjoy recreation or abstain from it. And they waste a lot of time in such choices; while they are worried about deciding which is better, they uselessly lose chances to do good things which would be far more to God's glory than this distinguishing between the good and the better (which has taken up their time) could possibly be.

We usually do not count small change; business would be too troublesome and would consume too much time if we tried to account for every nickel and dime in our pockets. And so we ought not to weigh every petty action to decide whether it deserves more time than something else. In fact, there is often a kind of superstition in trying to make such calculations. Why should we wonder whether it be better to hear Mass in one church than in another, to spin than to sew, to give alms to a woman than to a man? It is not good work to spend as much time in considering what needs to be done, as in doing the things that are done. We ought to proportion our attention to the importance of what we undertake. It would be unreasonable to take as much time preparing a one-day trip as a European vacation.

Choosing your vocation, seeking a spouse, planning some investment of great importance, or some work requiring a lot of time, moving to a new home, buying something very expensive, and the like deserve to be seriously pondered to see what is most in accord with God's will. But in dealing with little daily matters, in which even a mistake is neither important nor irreparable, there is no need to make them into a problem, to scrutinize them, to repeatedly ask advice about them. Why should I worry about whether God prefers for me to say the little office of our Lady or the rosary, whether I should go to visit somebody in the hospital or go to Vespers, whether I should go to hear a sermon or visit a church where there is an indulgence? Usually there is no difference between one such choice and another that makes any deliberation worthwhile. We have to proceed in good faith and without subtlety in this kind of consideration, and as St. Basil said, freely choose what we prefer in such a way as to not bore ourselves, not waste our time, and not risk anxiety, scruples, or superstition. Of course I am referring only to circumstances where there is no great difference between one choice and the other, and no serious imbalance between the two sides . . .

We should not doubt that it is good to carry out a decision like this that has been prayerfully made, for it cannot fail unless we fail. To do otherwise would be a sign of conceit, childishness, weakness, or silliness [book 8, chap. 14].

4. *The Holy Spirit worked in our Lady without any obstacle*

As we see a beautiful day break, not by jerks and shocks but by a sort of continuous brightening and swelling which is almost imperceptibly more perceptible, so that we truly see the day grow in light but so evenly that we do not perceive any interruption, separation, or discontinuity as it grows—thus divine love grew at every moment in the virginal heart of our glorious Lady, by sweet, peaceable, continuous growth, without any disturbance, shock, or violence at all.

No, Theotimus, we ought not to suppose that there was any rushing or forcefulness in the heavenly love of the Virgin's motherly heart; for love, of itself, is sweet, gracious, peaceful, and quiet. If it sometimes shoves, if it gives shocks to our spirit, this only happens because it encounters resistance. But when the passages of our souls are open to heavenly love without dispute or contradiction, it makes its way peacefully, with incomparable smoothness.

And so this holy love used its strength in the virginal heart of the holy Mother without any effort or rushing, because it found no resistance or hindrance whatever in her. For as we see great rivers foam and roar with loud noise in rough places where rocks make shoals and narrows that block and divert the current of the water, or on the other hand in level places, the same river flows and passes quietly without effort—so divine love, finding resistance and various hindrances in human souls (which everyone has to some degree but in different ways), does violence in such souls, fighting bad inclinations, beating on the heart, pushing the will by various disturbances and different efforts to get room for itself or at least to find some way around these obstacles.

But in the holy Virgin everything favored and supported the course of heavenly love. Its progress and increase in her were incomparably greater than in all the rest of creation, yet nevertheless sweet, peaceable, and quiet [book 7, chap. 14].

5. *The seven gifts of the Holy Spirit*

The Holy Spirit, who dwelleth in us, wishing to make our souls supple, pliable, and obedient, with regard to his heavenly movements and divine inspirations, which are the laws of his love, in the observance of which consists the supernatural felicity of this present life, bestows upon us seven properties and perfections, called, in the Holy Scripture and in the books of the theologians, gifts of the Holy Spirit.

Now, they are not only inseparable from charity, but,

all things well considered, and speaking precisely, they are the principal virtues, properties, and qualities of charity. For:

Wisdom is in fact no other thing than the love which relishes, tastes, and experiences how sweet and delicious God is;

Understanding is nothing else than love attentive to consider and penetrate the beauty of the truths of faith, to know thereby God in himself, and then descending from this to consider him in creatures;

Science or knowledge, on the other hand, is but the same love, keeping us attentive to the knowledge of ourselves and creatures, to make us re-ascend to a more perfect knowledge of the service which we owe to God;

Counsel is also love, insomuch as it makes us careful, attentive, and wise in choosing the means proper to serve God holily;

Fortitude is love encouraging and animating the heart, to execute that which counsel has determined should be done;

Piety is the love which sweetens labor, and makes us, with good heart, with pleasure, and with a filial affection, employ ourselves in works which please God our Father;

—and to conclude, Fear is nothing but love insomuch as it makes us fly and avoid what is displeasing to the divine Majesty [book 11, chap. 15]. «

Appendix IV

Freedom and Submission

There is a serious question underlying all that has been said in this book: how can human freedom be reconciled with our submission to God? We have spoken often about the need to be docile to God's will, to let ourselves be guided by the Holy Spirit, and so on. It can be objected that, in that case, we are merely puppets in God's hands. Where are our responsibility and freedom?

Such fear is false; it could even be the most serious temptation which the devil has used to separate people from God. On the contrary we should state firmly that *the more we are subject to God, the freer we are*. It could even be said that the only way we can win our freedom is by obeying God. This fact is hard to grasp and will always remain something of a mystery, but a series of points may help us understand why it is true.

1. Docility to God does not make us into puppets. Being guided by God's commandments and by inspirations of the Spirit does not mean "flying on autopilot" without having anything to do. It leaves room for us to exercise our full freedom, responsibility, initiative, and so on. But instead of the use of our freedom being random, or governed by our whims, God guides it in the way that is best for us. It becomes cooperation with God's grace,

cooperation that does not suppress but uses all our human faculties of will, intelligence, reason, and the like.

2. God is our creator, and it is he who holds us in existence as free beings at every moment. He is the source of our freedom; and the more dependent we are on God, the more that freedom flows forth from its source. Being dependent on another human being can be a limitation; but being dependent on God is not a limitation because there are no limits in God, who is infinite good. The only thing that he "forbids" us is what prevents us from being free, what prevents our fulfillment as people able to love and be loved freely, finding our happiness in love. The only limit that God imposes on us is the fact of being created. We cannot, without making ourselves unhappy, make of our lives anything other than that for which we have been created: to receive and give love.

3. What is freedom? It does not mean giving free rein to whim, but rather enabling what is best, most beautiful, and most profound in ourselves freely to emerge, instead of being stifled by more superficial things such as our fears, selfish attachments, or falsity. If we submit to God, that submission will in fact strip off a sort of shell that imprisons us, to make room for all that is genuine in us.

If we submit to God's will, it will certainly be opposed to part of ourselves. But this past is the negative part of us that limits us and from which God is gradually delivering us. God's will is never opposed to what is good in us: our aspiration to truth, life, happiness, and the fullness of love. Submission to God prunes things in us but never gets rid of the best that is in us: our deep, positive aspirations. Just the opposite: it awakens and strengthens them, orients them, and frees them from obstacles to their fulfillment.

4. This is confirmed by experience: people who go through life with the Lord and let themselves be led by him experience a growing feeling of freedom. Their hearts are not constrained or stifled, but expand and "breathe" ever more freely. God is infinite love; there is nothing narrow or confined about him. Everything in him is wide and spacious. Those who travel with God feel free; they feel that they have nothing to fear, that they are not subject to control, but on the contrary that everything is subject to them because everything works together for their good, whether favorable or unfavorable circumstances, good or bad. They feel that everything belongs to them because they are God's children; that nothing can limit them, because God belongs to them. They are not subject to conditions but always do what they want because what they want is to love, and that is always within their power. Nothing can separate them from the God they love; and they feel that even if they were in prison, they would be just as happy, because there is no way that any power in the world could take God away from them.

5. The real solution to the problem is not on the level of philosophy but in life as we live it. On the level of philosophy, we can always suspect there must be some

contradiction between our freedom and God's will. Ultimately, everything depends on how we situate ourselves in regard to God. Any opposition between our freedom and God's will is resolved completely if our relationship with God becomes a relationship of love, and it cannot be resolved in any other way.

When people love each other, they unite their wills freely and voluntarily and depend on each other; and the more closely they are bound to and depend on each other, the happier and freer they are. Adolescents are unhappy about being dependent on their parents, because that sort of dependence weighs them down; they would prefer to be autonomous and not to need anyone at all. But little children (and according to the Gospel we all need to become like that again) don't suffer because they are totally dependent on their parents, but just the reverse, because their dependence is an exchange of love. When they receive everything from their parents, it is actually their love that they receive and accept, and they respond to it by loving. Their way of loving consists of the joy of receiving, and turning what they receive into love.

6. All this means that if we want the (apparent) contradictions between God's will and our freedom to be resolved, we ought to ask the Holy Spirit for the grace to love God more, and the problem will solve itself. Loving God is the most demanding thing of all—it demands a total gift: you shall love the Lord your God with all your heart, with all your soul, and with all your strength. But at

the same time it is the least restricting thing of all: loving God is not a restriction, because his splendor and his beauty are so great that loving him is infinite happiness. God is infinite good, so that loving him does not constrict the heart but enlarges it infinitely.

On the other hand, if we were to lose this perspective of love, if the relationship between God and man were only a relationship of creator and creature, master and servant, and so on, then the problem would become insoluble. Nothing but love can resolve the contradiction between two freedoms: only love enables two freedoms to unite freely.

Loving means losing our freedom freely; but that loss is a gain, because it gives the Other to us and gives us to the Other. Loving God means losing ourselves in order to find and possess God, and ultimately finding ourselves in him. "He who finds his life will lose it, and he who loses his life for my sake will find it." [1] «

---

[1] Matthew 10: 39